Within the world are many worlds
and some are open, some are closed;
but ours was private, just for us.

COMBAT STRESS

Thanks to the kindness of the author, this edition of *A Private World* has been gifted to help the important work of Combat Stress, the Ex-Services Mental Welfare Society. Formed in 1919, the Society provides support, treatment and ongoing care for ex-Servicemen and women throughout Britain who are suffering from a combat-related psychiatric or stress disorder. Currently this means responsibility for almost 7,000 casualties of various campaigns, from 1939 through to recent conflicts in Northern Ireland, the Falkland Islands, the Balkans, Afghanistan, Sierra Leone and Iraq.

Each year, up to 860 individuals from Scotland, Northern Ireland and England, sometimes accompanied by family members, pass through Hollybush House respite and treatment centre near Ayr. A short stay there, in specialist hands, can literally be a life-saving experience for some; for all, including relatives and neighbours, there are many therapeutic benefits. The Society would be unable to provide such wide assistance without the generosity of the public and numerous major and smaller charities.

Clive Fairweather,
Scottish Appeal Director,
COMBAT STRESS,
Hollybush House,
Ayrshire KA6 7EA.

A PRIVATE WORLD

A Foot Soldier's Verses

David C. Simpson

EX-SERVICES MENTAL WELFARE SOCIETY

MMV

This edition of *A Private World*
is gifted by the author to the
charity Combat Stress on the basis of
'there but for the grace of God go I'.
A Private World incorporates *Interesting Times*,
published by The Ramsay Head Press in 2001.

A Private World can be ordered from
Combat Stress, Hollybush House,
Ayrshire KA6 7EA, Scotland.
Telephone 01292 560214

Published by Combat Stress, July 2005.
2nd Impression December 2005.

Printed and bound by
William Culross & Son Ltd.
Queen Street, Coupar Angus,
Perthshire PH13 9DF.
Tel: 01828 627266 Fax: 01828 627146

ISBN 0 9532791 2 X

Acknowledgements

I was greatly encouraged while I was trying to write these verses by the support I have been given by so many people. In particular, by my family, who took me seriously and never betrayed any surprise that I should start on what I was afraid would appear to them to be a daft-like project – far from that, they have given me great sympathy in my efforts to handle these memories, memories which have stayed fresh, perhaps too fresh, since my young days and which have refused to stay silent.

Poetry is a strange medium to try to handle when your career has moved in quite different fields and you come to it very late in life, and so there are two others to whom I am indebted and who deserve a very special mention: Anne Graham, playwright and Ann Rathie Guldberg, poet; they gave me support and confidence particularly when I was in two minds about the whole thing. I am also very grateful to Jennie Renton for her encouragement and very great help with production.

I would like to thank various individuals and official bodies for their kindness when I came to consider the illustrations to the collection; everyone was friendly, sympathetic and helpful. I am grateful to the Public Record Office at Kew for permission to reproduce extracts from the Battalion War Diary, and to the Crown Copyright Administor for permission to include extracts from the wartime 1:25,000 maps which we used in the fighting, and to the MOD Map Archive for copies of these maps. The wartime photographs which are included (except for the one of my platoon) are reproduced by courtesy of the Imperial War Museum, London, whose staff gave me assistance in tracking down sources. The post-war photographs were taken on my return visits. I am indebted to the Mansfield Traquair Trust and to Stanley J.W. Reilly for the use of his photograph of Phoebe Anna Traquair's Angel. The photograph of Derby Royal Infirmary is reproduced by kind permission of the Medical Illustration Services in that hospital.

I must also thank the Regimental Secretary of the Regimental Headquarters of The Royal Highland Fusiliers for permission to reproduce the crest of The Highland Light Infantry. The illustration on page 34 is from *Mountain and Flood* published by the 52nd (Lowland) Division History Committee just before the Division disbanded; and the illustrations on pages 44 and 56 from *The History of the 79th Armoured Division* published in 1945 just as it also was disbanding; my acknowledgements are due to these long-gone committees.

David Simpson

To Isobel,
who put me on my feet again,
and to whom I owe so very much

Preface

I feel very honoured to have been invited by Professor David Simpson to write an introduction to his second collection. I served alongside David in Holland and Germany in the 52nd Lowland (Scottish) Division and I feel a total empathy with his down-to-earth reflections on the day-to-day life of those workhorses of the battlefield, The Infantry. (It was Field Marshal Wavell who said: 'Always spell Infantry with a capital I.')

The author writes with absolute sensitivity, and without self-pity despite his almost fatal wounding over the Rhine. Nor does he hold any bitterness for friend or foe; indeed he has gone all the way by aiding a German charity.

After commanding a 30-strong Platoon of Glasgow Jocks and then as Battalion Intelligence Officer of the 5th Battalion The Highland Light Infantry, he has no difficulty in recording the whole gamut of emotions which befall the front line soldier – fear, comradeship and regimental pride, surely the primary factor in the 'Bash On Regardless' mentality which had perforce to encapsulate the 'Don't think ahead – it'll never happen to me' motifs which run through many of his verses.

I found this collection fascinating. It deserves a very wide readership – particularly by those 'who know not war'. They should be compulsory reading at the School of Infantry.

Frank Coutts, Brigadier (retired)
Platoon Commander,
4th Battalion The King's Own Scottish Borderers, 1944–45

Note

In all the accounts of engagements that follow, the contemporary War Diary method of reporting casualties has been used. That practice was to name officers and to give the total number of all other rank casualties (ORs) because its purpose was to report the consequent fighting capability of the battalion after it had been in action. The detailed reporting and naming of every individual casualty was of course recorded but through other channels. The casualty figures I give in footnotes under the verses only refer to the engagements mentioned in the verses and do not include those from other actions on other days.

The Verses

Introduction

When a watery sun broke through the clouds one day eight years ago, the change in the light suddenly carried me back over fifty years and I found myself lying on the steep slope on the side of a dyke in Beveland, seeing poor Harrison's face again. It was startling and totally unexpected and the images were not welcome but I found I had no option but to start writing about that morning there and then and I couldn't stop writing until I had the whole of 'Autumn Morning' down on paper.

The greatest difficulty in writing about those long past days lies in trying to convey to others the background to infantry life in the line and in particular that sense of being quite isolated from the rest of the world. Years ago I wrote, *'it was that morning that I had, for the very first time, a perception that the shelling and mortaring were not happening as an incident in my 'ordinary' life, but that I had somehow gone through a door out of the real world I knew, where that sort of thing couldn't happen, into a different, and separate, world where it could, co-existing in time but quite apart, where the rules were unknown but clearly very different'* – and, about being wounded – *'it was the first time that it had actually dawned on me that I might cross back into real life'*. I don't think I would like to alter a word of that.

Most of these verses are about situations which involved me when I was twenty-four, serving in North-West Europe with the 5th Battalion of the Highland Light Infantry, but a few relate to what happened to me after I was wounded there and came back to the UK. None of the events I selected were remarkable in themselves; instead they are typical of the sort of mess any infantry subaltern could have found himself in at that time. I would have found this period in my life very difficult to endure if it had not been for the great comradeship we shared, the very strong trust which existed between us, and our pride in 'our lot'.

I have tried to give an idea of my attitude of mind along with some of the rough humour we had, humour which helped us through the considerable amount of 'dirt, death and destruction' in our lives.

The figures I have given in the footnotes for the casualties incurred by our Battalion on the actual dates of each set of verses are there to keep the very real background to our life clearly in focus but, sadly, there were many other engagements with their own casualties.

It is often remarked that soldiers who were in the line don't talk about it. That is simply because we find it so difficult to explain the life we had to those who were not there. This is a feeble attempt to bridge at least some of that gap. As we used to say 'Over the bridge you go' 'But there isn't any bridge, Captain' 'Doesn't matter a b*****, over the bridge you go!'

D.C.S. 2005

Memories

Each year in turn steals a little from the newness of your youth
but in their footprints are held your memories of those passing times.
Sometimes the memories are gentle like those books on your shelves
which sit quietly there, waiting for you to take them down
and to read them again and to savour and to smile.

Other memories are restless and unquiet, they come uncalled and unwanted,
they make you play again their story, and it is hard to shut them out
even when you know only too well what happens at the finish.
The worst come stealthily, as dark shadows in the night when you are deep asleep
and then you find you are back – back living in those times, so long, so very long ago.

But then you awake and the quiet dawn light comes and the grey shapes go.
The bright colours of the sunlight give you back your own new comfortable shadows,
your own lively shadow for this present day and present time.
For a while you can live in your own today and are freed from your dark then
and the happy memories of your youth can return.

14 Platoon C Company of the 5th Battalion HLI relaxing after a period of 'informal training' with 15 Platoon on the moors in Scotland, early in May 1944 (when they had accidentally set the heather on fire with 2-inch mortar smoke bombs). All soldiers wore identity disks on string round their necks; these can be seen on a couple of men in the front row.

The Little World of Infantry

Within the world are many worlds
and some are open, some are closed,
but ours was private, just for us.
When others came to visit us
they never stayed for very long.

Though if there was a party on
the tanks and engineers and guns
would come and help and back us up,
but at the end they'd most return,
and let our frontiers close again.

Our country was a narrow band
that stretched away from flank to flank
sometimes it's deep, in places thin.
Its boundries, never fixed in space,
could ebb and flow and even break.

We lived in there with our own kind,
with dirt, and smells, in holes in ground,
and 'standing to' at dawn and dusk
and always, always, being alert
and checking each small thing we did.

The other people in our world
were soldiers living much like us
in thought and training and in aims,
but we were always facing them
and they were always facing us.

You could be in for days or weeks
without a break; but all that time
you knew those others facing you
would try to kill you if they could
so you must kill them if you can.

You only live from hour to hour,
no point in thinking of new day
for morning might not come for you,
you must respond as you were trained
and learn to walk each day with death.

Why were we there? – to hold, or push;
or when required to smash a gap
and tear right through and fix it proper
and keep things moving if we can,
before they settle back again.

And in this world you have to live
in dirty clothes with dirty feet
and far too often losing friends,
with time that never seemed to move
in days that never seem to end.

A pretty awful place you think?
A separate world cut off from life?
But here I learnt to my surprise
you still could find your spirits high,
could make a joke and raise a laugh.

Aardenburg Market, from Souvenir van Aardenburg, *which I picked up there in 1944.*

The 6th Battalion HLI had just fought their way across the Leopold Canal and were busy taking Aardenburg when, on 19/10/44, a few of us from the 5th Bn were sent up to the 6th for a couple of days' experience to see how it was going.

I suppose the clearing of that town was 'much as usual' with any small town, but naively I was totally unprepared for the reaction of a section of the townsfolk after the fighting was over. Aside from gross bullying, I had never, ever, imagined seeing women being treated so shockingly – having their heads shaved in vengeance, as a spectacle for the crowd.

We returned to the 5th Bn in good time for the crossing of the Scheldt and the assault on South Beveland.

Faces in a Small Crowd

I was up there with the 6th, up to see their attack – now that it was over I had no role.
Everything seemed quiet, the town cleared, firing stopped. I went out to look,
just to look about on my own as any armed visitor might risk in a newly freed town.
Then from the market came a noise of shouting and screaming so I went looking,
now looking to see, but still looking out. Most of the people were very quiet but
shouting was coming from a small crowd where four or five girls were standing,
just standing quietly there with shaven heads.

I stand still looking, still with my hand on my gun, still, just looking and feeling sick.
Slowly the people leave and those girls, the girls with the shorn heads, creep away.
Darkness falls and all is quiet but for a strange whining from many dynamo torches.
These people are tasting their own strange new freedoms,
freedom to move in the dark, freedom to speak out, freedom to decide,
now a brief freedom to settle scores. Freedom seems to mean so many things,
many more than I can understand.

I was only to be up there with the 6th for two days and now I am going back,
back down again to the 5th Battalion, back to my own platoon and to my own role.
A few days more and our battalion will be moving up, moving on in this Liberation thing,
and I think again about the girls, the shaven girls with those awful skulls,
bare white heads with white frightened faces, and about those others, the other faces there.
How many more shaven girls and gloating faces would I see,
shaven girls and those faces in a small crowd?

The British forces in Europe were called the British Liberation Army (BLA).

Troops being loaded into the Buffaloes of the 79th Armoued Division at Terneuzen 26/10/44.

We moved from Avelghem, in Belgium, to Hulst to prepare for the assault landing on South Beveland.

The day we were to move on from Hulst was a beautiful, sunny, autumn day and all the preparation was done. It was in the afternoon, while we were resting before the move and I was lying on the grassy ramparts of the town, that I experienced a quite extraordinary feeling of calm, an astonishing feeling under the circumstances. I felt as if the calm had been imposed on me from outside.

That evening we were transported up to Terneuzen on the south bank of the Scheldt, there to embark, be given our Mae Wests and loaded into the Buffaloes of the 79th Armoured Division, the 'funnies', which were to 'swim' us across the estuary.

I revisited South Beveland, Walcheron and Bergen-op-Zoom with my family in 1962 but not Hulst. I thought that if I went there the memory of that strange moment of peace would be lost and I was anxious to keep it – odd, isn't it.

Waiting at Hulst

I had told my Platoon what I knew of the plan,
(though that wasn't much, the way things were then).
I'd studied the maps – now had nothing to do
and that horrible business of waiting began,
it seemed quite unreal in the warmth of the sun.

But I lay on the grass in a quiet empty space,
and I found, where I lay, I was strangely at peace.
No thought for tomorrow or all that must come.
I had never expected to feel quite so calm,
tomorrow I knew we'd be facing a storm.

Then the waiting was done and that moment had gone
when early that evening we left that small town
for a little Dutch port on the banks of the Scheldt
and there we were loaded in strange-looking craft
that ferried us over to make our assault...

If I ever went back to that small pretty town
to look for that peace in the warmth of its sun,
(that curious peace that I'd happened upon)
my mind would be full of the men who had gone,
of the things we had seen and the things we had done.

I could never again find that circle of calm –
there are too many ghosts that refuse to lie down.

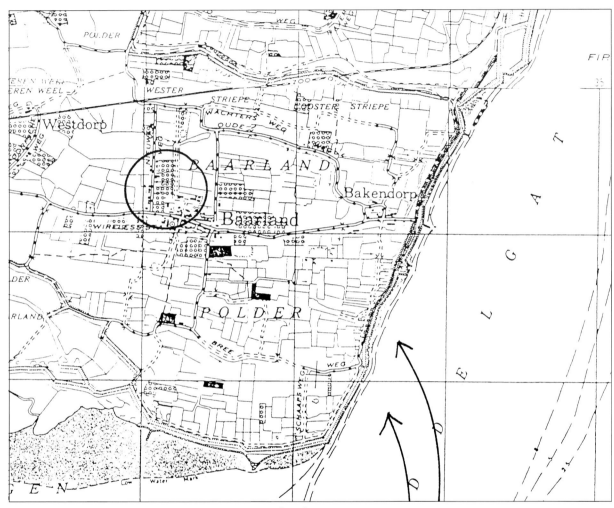

Baarland 27/10/44.
The circle on the map shows the orchard where we ate pears under mortar fire.

The Immaculate Major

We'd crossed the Scheldt, we'd climbed the dykes
and now were pinned by mortar fire,
caught in the orchard of a farm.
We lost some men and there we stuck
and ate the pears that lay in heaps
and felt the juice run down our chins.

That orchard though was full of threat
(the branches make the bombs explode
above you, as you're lying there),
so we pressed on and took that farm
and then we dug-in for the night
'consolidating', this is called.

Soon all was quiet and all was calm,
(but really rather bloody too
because, beside us, very dead
the cows and horses of the farm
gave out their own horrendous smell
that you could almost see and feel).

As darkness fell it rained and rained
and all the earth turned into mud
and water deepened in our pits.
I sent my sections each in turn
to have a brew-up in a house
so all the lads could keep alert.

Behind the pit that I had dug,
a table on two trestles stood
and on that table there was laid,
in formal state, with hands on chest
just like a bishop on his tomb,
a major of the German Reich.

I've often wondered who he was,
with his peaked cap and polished boots
and all his kit so very clean
so well turned-out in spite of rain,
and why on earth they'd laid him there,
so neat, so tidy, so alone?

There were so many questions here
like why was he so specially laid?
and if so special, why outside?
no other dead were laid like that
it left you wondering why, oh why?
and does he still stare at the sky?

Of course we had to leave him there
(he could have masked a booby trap),
but said goodbye to him at dawn
when we went off to push things on.
Poor chap, it hadn't been his day,
(but anyone could have bad luck).

5th Bn Cas. 27/10/44: 5 ORs killed in action, Lt J Pollock and 7 ORs wounded. (Lt J Pollock rejoined the Bn some time later but was killed in action on 22/1/45.)

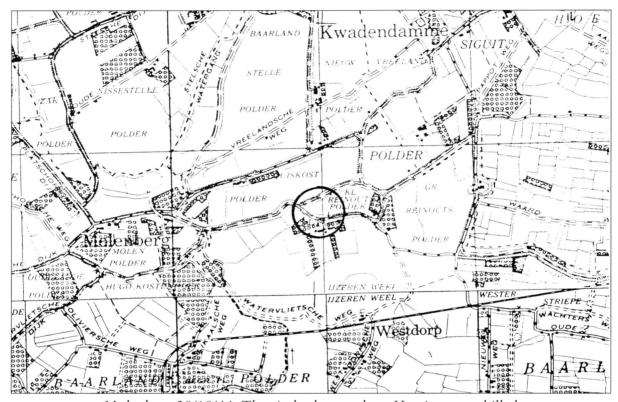

Molenberg 28/10/44. The circle shows where Harrison was killed.

The double lines on the map, which look like roads surrounding the polders, are actually dykes, each some ten to fifteen feet high. They were left-over stages from the historic recovery of the land from the sea – since the war some of these have been removed.

These dykes completely dominated the low flat polders which we had to cross and were a very unpleasant feature of the taking of Molenberg, on the left of the map.

Autumn Morning

It seemed too simple as we lay together, in early autumn sun
our shoulders touching and our bodies close.
My mind was filled with waves of sounds like angry bees
and tearing silk, like snapping wood and crackling fires.
Once again I said, go on, another go!

Next I must turn and look at our own quiet.
There seems to be a third eye there, but wet and red
near as no matter round an inch across,
(I'll close my eyes and see his face again)
well – *yes, it could have been a little less than that.*

I eased the Bren gun from his grasp and so we left him there alone
and went along the dyke. A field-grey figure raced for life
and cover of the trees across the flat. Revenge
should have felt better when I made that runner spin,
and fall, and lie as still, that second as the first.

You'll mind him fine. Harrison. He had that section's Bren.

And this was the start of that day.

28/10/44: Pte Harrison, 14 Pl C Coy 5th Bn HLI killed in action, Molenberg.
5th Bn Cas. 28/10/44: 6 ORs killed in action, Lt JF McFarlane (Bn SO) and 19 ORs wounded.

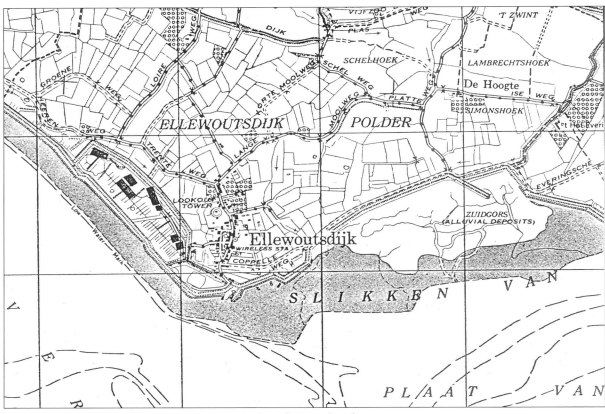

South Beveland

I don't know exactly where this happened but it was on a road in the southern part of South Beveland that we had to clear between 29/10/44 and 1/11/44. In retrospect I wonder about the 'tracked vehicle' – my memory is definitely that it had been tracked but I suppose it just might have been a very heavy truck with broad twin rear tyres.

Gemini

I suppose it must have been a tank or a half track,
it doesn't really matter, something heavy had rolled over them,
clearly something tracked, and so they must have lain there, those two flat soldiers,
lain till someone had pushed them off the road, off that road into our ditch,
these two sad cut-out figures that someone had just tossed out of their way.

They lie here in our cover, our path, in our ditch where we have to pass.
It takes us a moment to understand what they once had been,
now only cut-out cardboard figures in flat grey uniforms, flat and badly stained,
not with the clear cut edges that you might have expected,
but more fussy, blurred in an odd messy way and lying right in our path.

Like twins the two lie together, you can make out their forms as they lie still.
They look so alike, featureless but linked together as if in support,
strangely they seem to be at rest, their scream is quiet, its echo long gone.
Stupid to think, however we have no time to waste with nice feelings, or thinking,
no need either, no need, we can squeeze past, push them aside and pass easily.

Auf wiedersehen I thought as we went by.
Auf wiedersehen?

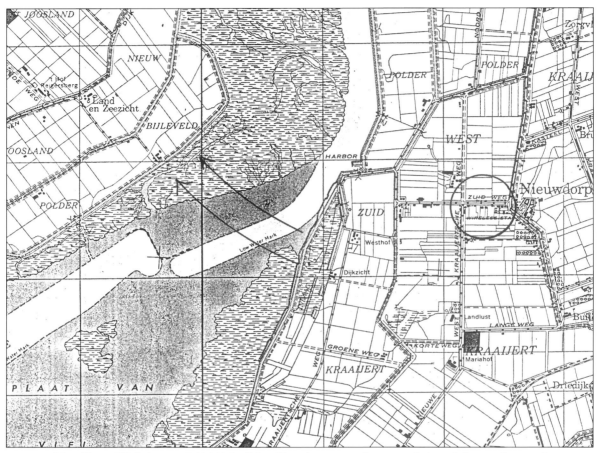

Het Sloe, Walcheren 3/11/44. (Het Sloe has now been reclaimed from the sea.)

Being told to take over Chris Ryde's job as Battalion Intelligence officer when he lost his leg meant that I had to say goodbye to my platoon and take over his I Section. Though I wasn't happy about losing my platoon, that was it and I just had to get used to it.

Plenty of Room Inside

The Boche had crossed and all was quiet
and we, for once, were sort-of safe;
we weren't to cross before first light
so we could rest on two and four
if we could find a quiet dry space.

So down the village street we squelched
in sodden boots, with weapons cocked,
until we found huge stable doors
belonging to a large Dutch barn,
undamaged, so it might be dry.

We burst the lock and in we went.
The night was dark but not as dark
as in that black and dismal place,
we crowded in and shut the doors
and then I risked a flash of torch.

As you'd expect I'd had some scares
and now was used to horrid sights
but what appeared from out the dark,
with giant shadows at its back,
was straight from Edgar Allan Poe.

It towered above us like a threat,
some ten feet high with all its urns,
a box of ebony and glass
with silver trim, on giant wheels
and shafts which vanished to the roof.

Short posts stuck out from further walls
on which the harness sadly hung,
all silver buckles and black plumes,
a ghastly ancient horse-drawn hearse,
all ready for its next dead man.

Though deeply shocked I had to laugh
(to make it funny for the men)
and on we went to further barns.
We needed rest before we crossed
and faced the usual chance of death.

Next dawn we slithered in the mud,
then down the dykes and in the boats
and up more dykes which had been mined,
and poor old Chris blew off his leg
and I was told to take his job.

5th Bn Cas. 3–4 Nov '44: Lt A K Solbu and 2 ORs killed in action, 2 ORs drowned, 5 ORs missing, Lt Chris B Ryde (Bn IO) and 8 ORs wounded. (Lt AK Solbu was one of the Norwegian officers which were attached to the Division when our role had been the invasion of Norway.) The mines which had been laid along the dykes were Schuh mines – small wooden boxes with hinged lids, filled with explosives; the only metal part was the detonating mechanism – very cheap and very nasty.

The convent in Bergen-op-Zoom.

After the fighting in South Beveland and Walcheron, we were brought back to Bergen-op-Zoom to make good our losses in men and equipment. Being billeted there in a convent was an extremely strange experience – but taking this photograph was also pretty odd.

It is a real 'what happens next' photograph. I took it in 1962 and it turned out to be the last negative on my film. The man crossing the road was being rather inquisitive – I think he wondered why I should be photographing the convent and in turn, the woman on the bike was wondering what he was looking at.

Then the man, who was still staring at me, walked into the bike.

A Meditation from a Nun's Cold Bed

When all our Boche were carted off
they brought us back to re-equip
and dumped us in a little town
where all the civvies had returned
(it lay some way behind the lines).

The men lived in a Wehrmacht camp,
and (*really quite the oddest twist*)
the officers in a Convent House,
so every time we came or went
a convent sister checked us out.

Above the hall that was our Mess
there ran a quite enormous room,
a dormitory for novice nuns
and that was where I had my bed,
some five foot six of sleeping space.

Partitions split that freezing barn
into maybe thirty 'rooms';
thin curtains screened their open sides
and you could stare up from your bed
and count the rafters in the roof,

and it was cold, so very cold.

While I lay there, in 'my' nun's bed,
I felt concern for that young nun,
was she at peace within this place?
I wondered what it must be like
to live your life in such chill gloom.

Her tiny world was set with ties
that bound her to that small cold bed,
her life imprisoned by these walls,
a life of service in cold quiet,
of hidden prayer, devoted love.

And from her bed my heart went out
to that strange girl, whose heart was here,
I prayed she loved her way of life,
had her reward in peace and prayer,
could see beyond cold Convent walls.

She must have been an age with me
and so she may be living still,
still in that cold and gloomy house.
I often think about that bed
where our two worlds did coincide,

where it was cold, so very cold.

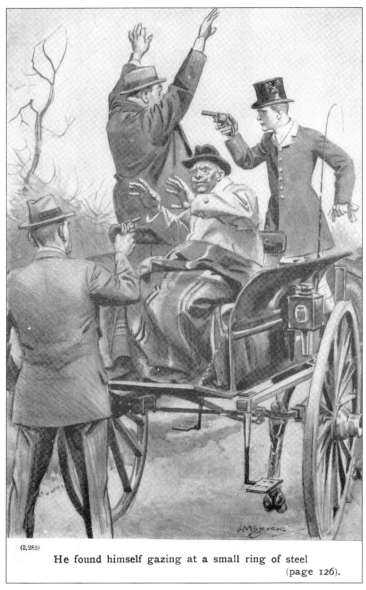

(2,283)

He found himself gazing at a small ring of steel
(page 126).

From PJ, the Secret Service Boy *by Lord Frederick Hamilton.*

This 'Boy's Adventure Story' was published c. 1922 Thomas Nelson and Sons, Ltd.

There was also a sequel – *More about PJ, the Secret Service Boy.*

Another 'super' writer of boy's adventure stories when I was young was Percy F. Westerman. He was a prolific writer of rattling good tales of dare-devil adventures, all ripping yarns.

Ripping Fun

When I was eight, I used to read
beneath the sheets in my small bed,
adventure tales and ripping yarns
of first class shows with British boys
defeating foreigners with ease,
boy heroes winning in the end.

When I was twelve I knew full well
that British boys were quite the best,
the envy of each foreign race,
clean fighters each and every one
who stood for all that's good and fine
and loved to have such ripping fun.

Some twelve years on, or thereabouts,
I found myself a soldier boy
soldiering in a foreign land,
but now you see I'd quite grown up.
I didn't find it all that fun,
more death and losing pals and stuff.

I think, if you had asked us then,
we'd say the way we looked at it
was fighting battles was a job,
a job which we were good at doing
and had great pride in what we did,
we rarely saw it as a game.

It could be simply, we were there,
and if we'd been some way away
we might have seen it differently.

Yes,
maybe we were rather close
to catch the spirit of the thing.

On 21/11/44, while we were getting back to Battalion strength after Beveland/Walcheron, we had a visit from someone from 'high up' who said how proud he was of us, and who told us that he had asked Monty and Monty had promised that we wouldn't be used again in an action until there was another 'first class show' for us.

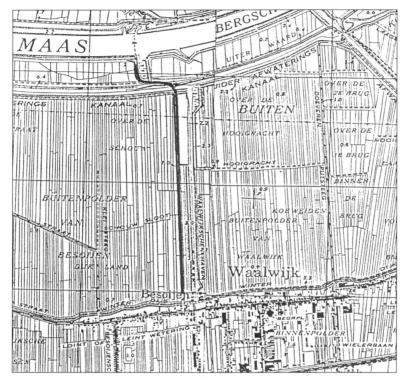

Waalwijk 30/11/44.

The Battalion positions were along the line of the small town of Waalwijk which stood behind the ridge of a flood dyke. To our north, the land, divided by countless drainage ditches, was flat and wet and bare. The enemy held the north bank of the Maas and all the country to the north of that.

The *'hellish road'* was actually 2km long and ran due north from Waalwijk to the river and a ferryman's house – the line of the road has been emphasised on the map. The *'huge church tower'* of Waalwijk church was over 110 feet high and its seven shaky ladders took us to the top to spy on the enemy across the Maas. The flat land between us meant that they too could spy on us from water towers – hence the problem of that dreadful *'dead straight'* road.

Looking for Laurie

The dawn was red when I turned back,
without succeeding in my task,
but now it's day and bright and clear,
too clear, too late, along the road
that runs dead straight from them to us.

They surely must be now alert
and looking out and 'standing to',
my road is fully in their sight
but will they shoot, or play that game
where you could nearly make it home?

I do not know but have to try
and feeling naked and afraid,
I pace best speed but do not run,
they have to think that I am theirs,
so they can almost let me win.

There is no choice of route or time,
my road is this, no time but now
while early sun dries off the dew
and picks me out and warms my face
and lights the church and little town.

That lies ahead, in sleep-like death,
no smoke, no sound, no sign of life
and, rising up, the huge church tower
spies out the empty, empty land,
so wet, so flat, so cold, so dead.

I walked along that mile-long road,
which ran beside a half-filled ditch,
a barren place, no cover there
and all that walk I knew full well
that right behind lay threat of death.

My friends could see me on that road
and I too knew they watched for me
but they were helpless, as was I
and had to trust in faith and hope
but no shells came and I won back.

So live I did. Now years have past,
these many years, much love, much death,
and in my mind that road goes on,
that hellish road, that testing mile,
with mouse and cat, and sweating palm.

(It takes its place with other dreams.)

Lt JLS (Laurie) Watson was killed in action whilst on night patrol on the banks of the Maas on the night 29/30 Nov 1944 – his body was not found by the subsequent patrols sent out that night to look for him and indeed it was not found and recovered till the night of 2/12/44.

A V2 rocket, still on its trailer, being elevated into position for launching.
(Imperial War Museum negative no. BU10762)

From the Battalion's positions on the south bank of the Maas, we could see trails of the V2 rockets being launched from across the river and away to the north.

Seeing a newly launched V2 rocket vanishing into the clouds on its way to Britain was an extremely strange and a very horrid experience for me because my sister was working in a hospital in London at that time.

The rocket launchers were all out of our range but we reported back the bearings of every one we saw – however, there was no cross-bearing and the units themselves could vanish just like the trails.

Each Twisted Trail

The little pointy ghost rises slowly,
far beyond our reach, across that river,
maybe five miles away, maybe more.
The vapour trail it leaves behind is not straight,
not hanging straight below, but twisted,
crumpled like a bit of loose string.

As it rises higher, its trail straightens,
hanging from that tiny dot in the sky.
Soon the pointed tip escapes from view.
vanishing suddenly into the dark cloud.
Now there is just the flat bleak land,
a ghost of twisted trail and the dark grey sky.

Those thin remains of the rocket's trail
will hang there for a few brief moments.
Soon they too will go and then only emptiness,
only the bitter coldness of this cold wet country.
In five or six minutes time, quite suddenly,
there will be more death in London.

A massive German Eagle perched on its Swastica.

We visited the huge stadium built for the 1938 Nazi Party Rally at Nuremberg a few days before Hitler arrived and the huge Rally began. My memories of Nuremberg are of long banners, public address loudspeakers on all the lamp-standards and of the marching cohorts of the brown-shirted Stürmabteilung (SA) and the black-shirted Schutzstaffel (SS).

*'The three of us' on the garden steps of Pension Heim-am-See at
Rottach-Egern, on the Tegernsee, in August 1938.*

Die Braunkohle

The sudden shaft of winter sun
lit up the empty frontier post
while we, and all our lot, rolled past;
most never noticed that we'd gone
into the land of Hitler's Reich,
(mind you, to me, it looked the same
as other countries we'd gone through)
but, when we'd gone a hundred yards,
I smelt that thrilling German smell
that comes from burning their brown coal.

One breath of that was all it took
to take me back six years or more
and I was standing on a peak
and soaking up Bavarian sun
above the lake of Tegernsee.
There'd only been the three of us,
(one dead, one crashed in flames, one left)
we climbed, we sailed, we drank the beer
and surfed behind a speeding boat
and it was absolutely great –
but when our time down there was up
we went through cities going home
and there we saw the other side
the cruelty and the evil side,
the real face of that Master Race.

I rubbed my eyes and I was back
in drab December 'forty-four.
I never told my army pals,
for which of them would understand
the magic brown coal held for me?

'Brown coal' was Lignite, a soft coal which burned with a strong smell rather like peat.
I think that this particular frontier post was at the border just outside Sittard in the Netherlands.

Hochheid 34, bei Geilenkirchen

The '*smart new modern house*' photographed in 1987, with its roof now all made good and no sign of that hole. The occupants very kindly took me up to the attic and down into the cellar, a rather creepy experience.

A Bit of a Baur

On the edge of our own wood
there stands a smart new modern house
but what I found attracted me
was quite a large and ragged hole
that sadly spoilt its red tiled roof.

So when I thought I'd like a view
I'd climb up there to have a look,
a cautious keek as you'd expect,
the other lot who'd made the hole
were likely to be looking too.

We were the right of our 12th Corps
and on our right flank were the Yanks.
Supporting them, far to their rear,
their batteries of huge great guns
for taking on the Siegfried Line.

One day their major came to call,
(he wanted something small to hit
to check how accurate they were)
and off we went upstairs to spy
and see what needed to be done.

I pointed out some funny things
and these he kindly blew to bits
with shells that roared and screamed above,
then, from the dust and smoke and flame,
two German Staff cars scurried out!

We stared – we laughed, but they well knew
that someone had controlled these shells,
and thought the house a likely post,
so when we stopped to check our maps,
the attic filled with small arms fire.

Well – we were being relieved next day,
the major'd finished checking guns,
so, laughing still, we came downstairs.
We wondered who'd been in those cars –
and if they'd liked being in the line.

I thanked him for a lovely day
and he went off to tell his boys.
(I*n Bonn in 1973*
I met a man who had been there –
and there we two drank Bruderschaft.)

5th Bn Cas. 27/12/44–1/1/45: 3 ORs killed in action, Lt Durrell and 19 ORs wounded.

'Baur': a joke, esp. a robust joke – Scots.
Bruderschaft trinken: to pledge close friendship.

'With dirt, and smells, in holes in ground' (p.3)

One of the Battalion's weapon pits (slit trenches) at the north end of the wood at Hochheid, dug about Christmas 1944, as it appeared some forty years later.

Grey Shapes and Short Eternities

It's an hour before the dawn and we are looking out for grey shapes,
looking out for field-grey shapes moving through the pitch dark.
We are 'standing to' and listening and staring out at all those dark shapes
and all the other black shapes that could, or might, have moved
but it's the grey shapes really, we are really only looking out for grey shapes.

It's an hour before dawn and everything is very dark
all shades of black under a deep black winter sky.
Slowly, heavily, it changes and now we can look out for grey shapes in a dim grey light.
Quite suddenly, to my own relief, a faint and thin washed colour starts to grow
but still we are only looking out for grey shapes.

At last that long dark hour has gone and we 'stand down'
and now, in due order, we prepare for all the dangers of that new bright day
(but still we always keep an eye alert for grey shapes).
So it is with each and every dawn – and so in turn with each and every dusk;
I suppose a kind of Matins and a Compline if you're with that sort of thing.

(I think that I may always be looking out for grey shapes.)

'[Infantry] … must "stand to" an hour before daylight and an hour before dusk and remain standing
to until ordered to stand down.' *Infantry Section Leading* Chap. X.74.3.vii (p.71), HMSO, 1938.

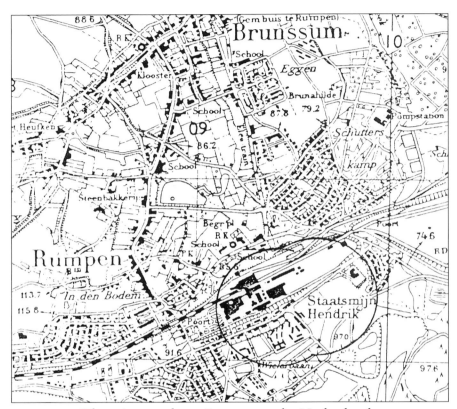

The mine works at Brunssum, the Netherlands.

'*Top Secret*' was used, not because of the contained message but because of the 'distribution' which was in effect a list of most of the units in the Brigade that might be caught starkers at Brunssum that day!

An Odd Thing

You would have thought we would have liked it, us living as we were
and surely, after all that dirt, it would have been great
and surely no one, no nice person, could have liked being like that
but of course, you see, we were used to it, we were all of us used to it
and after all those weeks we had got used to being used to it;
we didn't mind being like that, after all it was what we were all used to.

And then into this world came a coded message, 'Top Secret', written in code
(wet paper read in a muddy trench, soft wet paper with mud from muddied hands)
so we didn't have an option, no choice at all, it was an order like any other.
We were pulled out of the line and waited there, waited till they came to take us,
loaded now in big troop transporters, grubby soldiers with their odd good smell;
soldiers still with smartly shaven faces, above uniforms now worn as a second skin.

We weren't surprised when we reached the mines at Brunssum
and were sent into the big black dirty buildings. The Bath Unit men divided us,
the men were sent off to the showers, the officers to the Direktor's baths
and the kind Bath Unit men gave us clean shirts and vests and pants and socks
but only in exchange for our nice old ones we had been wearing for a lifetime,
only then could we run the baths, that was one thing for us, we ran our own baths.

Lying in a hot bath in a chilly cubicle anywhere, you could be anywhere, it's magic.
While you are there you are not going anywhere, you are safe and you believe it,
others are looking out for you and you are quite secure and not going anywhere,
but that won't last and it doesn't – and so you dry and put on your new clothes,
the new vest and pants and socks and that new shirt you were given by the Bath man,
but the shirt smells queer with an odd smell. *Just like a wee chemist's shop*, you say.

And the men from the Bath Unit just laughed. Oh that's just the DDT they said
and then they laughed again and the new shirts were like in the films, with no tails,
back or front, just buttoning right down the front, no tails like British shirts –
and the Bath Unit men laughed again, they just laughed and said Fancy you grumbling
but tails are good each day when you have to go and there is no cover and
of course we grumbled, no tails back or front, that funny smell and their laughs.

Then we went out into the cold, that bitter cruel cold we lived rough in
and there seemed to be no warmth in these new clothes, the new clean clothes,
we knew it would take a week before the clothes even began to get nice and greasy
and good and comfy and warm, warm with sweat and grease like our old clothes
and we forgot about those baths and being clean and we went back up to the line,
 grumbling, clean but grumbling, us with our new smell just like a wee chemist's shop.

'... in such a field are nightmares made... and still you have too far to go.'

This photograph was taken in 1987 looking over from the start line at Tuddern across a 2 km. field to Havert, Lind and Stein lying behind the Saeffeln Beck. That was an anti-tank, water-filled ditch, about 6 metres wide. The church of Havert is on the skyline on the left.

This attack was at the start of Operation Blackcock, to clear a large pocket of the enemy from the west side of the river Roer. It lasted just over a week, during which our Division, the 52nd Lowland, lost 101 officers and men killed and 752 others wounded. It prompted a change in the allocation of Battalions to Brigades, in order to spread casualties over different pre-war Territorial Army recruitment areas in the future.

The Fine Fabrics Department

When you are used to living rough,
a ruined house spells luxury,
especially if the roof is fair
and if the beds are not too bad
and you can get a bit of kip.

So when we moved to Hillensberg
to form up for the next 'big push',
it went down well with one and all
to have some comfort for a night,
and shelter from that dreadful cold.

Mine-clearing tanks were grouping too
(they came up from a base behind)
but our main street was far too steep
and they went sliding down the hill,
now just a sheet of glistening ice.

We helped them on by throwing out
the village bedding we could spare
(all quilts and curtains, sheets and rugs)
so now their tracks could get a grip
and off they went to wait for us.

That night there was a bitter frost,
as hard as any that we'd had,
and as the dawn came up next day,
from black to grey, from grey to bright,
the village looked like fairyland.

Those dirty blankets and the rags
had been transformed by that hoar frost,
now finest velvet fills the street
and damask linen, cashmere shawls
and bales of silk are strewn about.

Too soon the wintry sun comes up
too soon the velvet disappears
and we have filth and dirt again,
but, worse than that, the thaw goes on
the ground grows soft beneath our feet.

That night we moved up for the Start
at dawn we formed the second wave
to cross a field of thawing mud
and from the far side came bad news,
the tanks were stuck and mines not cleared.

In such a field are nightmares made
when red hot splinters fly about
and down you go in frozen slush
and smoke and wreckage haze your view,
and still you have too far to go.

But at the end of that long day
when I could find some time to think –
the image that came back to me
was not just mud or death or screams
but silk and damask and cashmere.

5th Bn Cas. 18/1/45: 12 ORs killed in action, 31 ORs wounded.
'Mine-clearing tanks'… 79th Armd Div's Crabs – Shermans fitted with a rotating flail.

'... and what about that village shrine?'

Bashing-On Regardless

Amongst the trees that line the road
a simple shrine serenely stands
and from His cross between two trunks
the sadden'd Christ looks down below
on *Everyman* – who passed Him by.

The little village lies outstretched
across the open snowy ground
its houses black against the sky,
each with its garden at the back
with hut and fruit trees and its hedge.

So, very pretty it may look
except, of course, for what goes on,
the little figures run, some fall,
some fire their guns or throw their things
or just stay lying deep in snow.

That lovely whiteness soon is spoiled
with giant spreading ink-blot stains
and from the gardens on the right
two Sherman tanks brew up in flames,
as if an ancient Hindu pyre.

But in this picture you can't see
there's all the colour brought by noise,
the whine of mortar, screech of shell
and loud explosions, small arms fire,
the roar of flames from burning homes.

In two short hours our five are killed
and seventeen more are wounded here.
That village now is just a wreck
but, they are out and we are in,
one village gone, one less to take.

In those two hours it's all forbye
and I'm left thinking of two pals,
the first one's head was neatly split
by airburst shell, from crown to jaw,
the second wounded but still lives.

And as I brew my tea (with rum),
I think about the day's events
and, though I know it couldn't be,
I feel the odds are shortening down,
and what about that village shrine?

5th Bn Cas. 22/1/45: Laffeld, 1500–1700hrs – Lt J Pollock and 4 ORs killed in action. Capt R Baird and 16 ORs wounded.

If a tank goes on fire it 'brews-up'; these two Sherman tanks had been Crocodiles (flame throwing tanks – more 79th Div funnies), which had been knocked out by a German Tiger tank.

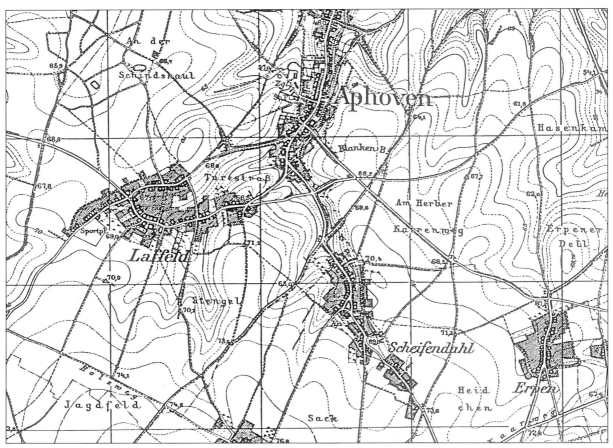

The assault on Laffeld was mounted from the west on 22/1/45 – it was all over in two hours. The snow lay on the ground and it was very cold.

*'The little village lies outstretched
across the open snowy ground'*

A Brief Reflection

It was sad that there was no clear end.
A cold winter's day – like all the others then.
As usual, you had wondered about yourself,
would you be there at the end of the day?
But you didn't dwell on that for long –
it didn't do to think about that at all.

Anyhow, as I said before, no clear end,
no clear cut end to that friendship of ours.
At the start he was, then at the end he had gone,
that was all, at the other side of that village,
quite near really, not far away from where I was,
somewhere near in that noisy snowy hell.

When I heard about him we'd moved on,
now out at the other end of the village.
Anyway you couldn't go back, you went on,
you, with all the others, playing out your role,
we were still moving on, you see,
we were pressing on towards Aphoven.

* * * * * *

I was sad about my friend,
and I never saw his body…
I only heard that he'd gone,
so I never said good-bye.
Now little time to think of him,
and tomorrow will be today again.

* * * * * *

Of course any tomorrow could be yours.
Life was a bit like that, then.

Kirkhoven 25/1/45.

When I had that '*mug of tea*' I had been through a difficult day. Our battalion had attacked Kirkhoven (1 killed in action, 4 wounded), but I had been in another battalion's dusk assault on Heinsberg, travelling as a liaison officer in one of the 79th Armoured Division's Sherman Tanks. There is very little room in a Sherman, all needed for its own crew, so I had to be fitted in, lying under their gun – just where a Tiger's shell might be expected. When the assault was over I had then to make my way back in the pitch black to my lot, the 5th Bn HLI, in Kirkhoven – quite on my own, through the town, with the odd burning house.

I'm afraid my sense of humour was not up to it that night when, as Bn IO, I came back to my sad responsibility of writing up the battalion's casualties for the day for the War Diary – and then someone gave me a letter from the Inland Revenue.

My tea was not from the army ration Tea/Sugar/Milk Powder but from a real tea bag sent by a cousin in Canada, and brewed on a Tommy cooker with a Meta fuel tablet.

The Tax Man Reacheth Out

You lived in quite a different world
where nothing really was the same,
you lived and slept in all your clothes,
you lived and slept in muddy holes
and ate when it was safe to do
from rations from a ration pack
each with supplies for fourteen men
(including fags and boggy-bumf)
and if you were a lucky boy
your letters came up with those packs
with news from home, that other world.

One night, when I'd been very pushed
and had a nasty stretch of risk
and managed at the end to find
a little comfort in a house,
I brewed a mug of tea (or char)
with just a drop of rum (no milk)
and thought about the next day's task
and counted up the men we'd lost
and all that sort of detailed stuff.
I had a letter in the mail
a letter from the Income Tax.

I really think I'd better stop.
(I cannot find the proper words
for what I think I want to say).

The idea of angels has been familiar to me all my life. This is one of four painted by Phoebe Anna Traquair in the murals on the chancel arch of the Mansfield Place Church in Edinburgh and I remember looking up at them when I was a very small boy. To me they are the definitive depictions of angels.

The image of a ripple running through the clouds is now familiar from films of atomic explosions. But in Heuman in February 1945, while we were preparing to take part in Operation Veritable, the huge ripple that crossed the low cloud above our heads was an extraordinary sight. I guessed it had been caused by a heavy bombing raid, but that didn't stop me from thinking about the Angel of Mons.

That thought was strangely comforting to me when we went into the assault the next day for 'our next push', a major Army operation with the objective of clearing the enemy from the SW banks of the Rhine, which was achieved by 10/3/45. During it, our Bn lost 24 killed or missing, and 47 wounded.

The Angel

I had no warning.
Of course I'd heard about it,
but never really believed.
A legend from the first war, folk-lore.

The Yanks had relieved us for our next push –
in darkness we left our bank of the Maas,
silently – (enemy listening on the other bank).
Then we travelled north all night.

At dawn we arrived here,
to prepare for tomorrow.
Towards evening I looked to distant woods,
thinking about that.

Then there was a deep rumble from the east,
a heavy bombardment.
I looked up to sense our weather
as a great wave ran through clouds above me.

The huge silent ripple rushed through those clouds
and I remembered the Angel of Mons
and I was still, quite still,
thinking what dawn would bring.

(Ages since sleep)

I was grateful for that thought of the Angel.
The thought came with me in the morning,
I thought of that Angel as we went up.

A royal flush – Ace, King, Queen, Jack and Ten of the same suit of cards. The 'cards in question' were not, of course, these modern ones but the more florid continental ones then in use in Germany.

Our rather black sense of humour at that time was one of the things that kept us going, and this *was* funny. However, I suppose it is *just* possible that one of the lads of the leading company might have added the extra card and upgraded the hand to a royal flush when taking a brief cover from the enemy mortaring we were having as we reached the edge of the wood. We were close behind and I very much doubt that there was either the time or the opportunity. But who knows?

As We Came Up

One day we had to take a wood,
(I always hated being in woods,
that threatening gloom beneath dark trees
and mortar bursts above our heads)
and as we came up to its edge
we saw dead Germans in their pits,
killed by the shells that came from guns
supporting us as we came up.

My attitude of mind was odd
while I was living in those times,
I never really came to terms
with how things were in life outside,
that life we'd left so far behind
and what was right in our strange World,
that new and very different world
that separate world where we now lived.

And so for us, as we came up,
within that frame of mind we had
in times like this, it suited well
to see dead Germans in their pits,
a simple case of them or us.
One trench was different, with four lads
killed in their pit while playing cards,
caught by surprise with the attack.

As we came up to that wood's edge,
we saw those soldiers in that pit
and had to laugh – that may sound strange
(for we ourselves were under fire).
Three of the four were knocked about,
the fourth one too was very dead
but in his hand a royal flush!
We had to laugh, when we saw that.

He should have won but we came up,
and that's just life, or death perhaps?
They weren't expecting an attack –
a piece of really rotten luck
that we came up to that wood's edge
and took the wood and all that ground
and spoilt their game and moment's peace,
and spoilt the players playing too.

When we went past I'd had to laugh,
that Royal Flush was much too much,
it seemed so funny at that time.

Those years have gone,
my world has changed.
It did seem funny at the time.
I'm not so sure it's funny now.

Broederbusch – 'a very evil threatening wood'.

A Thought

It's very odd, (but there it is)
it only happened just that once,
(and why it did I do not know)
as we went up to take that wood,
(a very evil threatening wood)
and 'move the battle on a bit'.

A battery of forward guns
were firing when we passed on through.
We came quite close and gunners waved,
and now I think I read their thoughts
of 'there they go – the PBI' and
'rather them going there than us'.

And then I thought – (I shouldn't tell)
I thought – but only just that once,
I thought the thought you mustn't think
of why, of why it's always us?
and not these gunners? – or Brigade?
or any other lucky sods?

Then on we went into the game
with airburst shells and open rides
between the lines of threatening gloom
and metal screamed and men were killed.
That thought was gone and I was back
in country that I understood.

It only happened just that once
and why it did I do not know
because for me I always found
a mad contentment in my job
with trust in friends and pride in jocks
and in the battle role we played.

It only happened just that once –
but why that day I do not know.

5th Bn Cas. 16/2/45: 1300–1800hrs – 4 ORs killed and Lt J Browne & 32 ORs wounded.
(PBI = Poor Bloody Infantry.)

Kasteel Blijenbeek and moat, 1987.

Really Bloody Bad Luck

The first time you come under fire
your training helps you to survive
and if you've been to Battle School
the terrors of the battlefield
have noises that you've heard before.

In January of '44
I'd been through various sorts of hell
through water, smoke and DM gas
in battle kit, with all the while
explosions and machine gun fire.

The chap who drove us all so hard
and made us sweat and run up hills
and throw ourselves on Danert wire
as bridges for the other lads,
he'd lash us with his caustic tongue.

The campaign ribbon that he wore
gave him an extra sort of power.
It seemed so right to hate this man
but now I'm sorry that I did,
because his training served me well.

Some twelve months after I'd been there,
when we were making a new line,
some reinforcements came at dusk
and in that group, to my surprise,
I saw the chap I'd hated so.

But things are very different now
and so I went and welcomed him
and while we chatted there I found
that he had never fought before
and this for him was his first time.

Then off he went to see the Adj.
to learn from him just where to go.
I wished him luck as he went off.
I never saw that chap again,
for he was killed that night, you know.

So that was it,
and that was that,
like so much else,
within that private world of ours.

5th Bn Cas. 25–26 Feb '45: Kasteel Blijenbeek, Lt Sharp and 2 OR killed in action, 2 OR wounded and 14 OR missing.

'Danert wire' was the name of the large coils of concertina barbed wire, usually used as three coils, one on top of two others and stretched out as a defence line.

German Self-Propelled 88mm gun.

'but pretty soon came under fire, too close for comfort...'

A Nice Quiet Day

We were ready 'for what comes'
whatever that might prove to be,
and didn't have too long to wait
before the order from on high
came calling Rhoddy to Brigade,
and as his IO, I went too.

Division hadn't yet told Brigade
exactly what's *our* task ahead;
but waiting there I found *their* loo,
the first I'd seen for quite some weeks,
it barely worked, a feeble flush,
some kind of omen? I hoped not.

Div's plan for us, when it came down,
was we 'would make a night attack
in five hours time' (for it was late)
'and flush the Germans from our bank'.
Our CO had to hurry back
to plan and call his 'O' group in.

He told them what we had to do,
and when and how, and all that stuff
about that barrage from Div's guns
and times for this and times for that
and what was known about the troops
(about the enemy and us).

That night was really very dark,
no light to help us move about.
It rarely came as black as this;
though that was good for our attack,
on pitch dark nights, troops can get lost,
(a rather terrifying thought).

The Army solves this with white tape,
white tape that reaches on and on.
The tape is laid in no-man's land
to show the line of the advance.
The IO lays it with his men
and heaven help him if he's wrong.

So off they go into the black
with these great rolls of white, white tape,
to go as far as they *must* go,
then roll it out on their way back,
but pretty soon come under fire
too close for comfort, there they pause.

Those rounds are followed by a flare
and as they look up from the mud
they see the spot they're heading for
and start the laying, just in time
to finish off that scary job,
make home before the barrage drops.

But when those shells begin to land,
they aren't as far in front, as planned,
some shells come down a deal too near,
in fact on top of some of us.
A nasty jolt for all the men
as we move off in our attack.

In clear, the CO swore *on air*
and told the gunners what to do.
'Code *must* be used' – replied Brigade
(but then, you know, *Brigade weren't there*).
Quite soon we found our foe had left,
so it turned out a nice quiet day.

5th Bn Cas. 10/3/45: 5 ORs wounded.
Rhoddy – Lt-Col RLC Rose DSC, MC – CO 5th Bn HLI.
The CO's 'O' (Orders) Group consisted of the Bn 2i/c, the Coy Commanders and Adj, IO etc.
The 'barrage' was meant to support us and came from an AGRA, Army Group Royal Artillery.

Although

You knew,
of course you knew, you'd be alright,
in spite of all that nearly stuff
and all the times that they'd just missed
with things that came with hellish noise,
the airburst shells, explosion blasts,
in spite of these, you think you know,
most times you know you'll be alright...

Your life goes on, from hour to hour,
from here to there or then till now,
you mostly think you're doing fine
(though being scared from time to time).
You cease to think about Outside,
you've come so far, so what the hell,
you just go on, though now you think
it's likely that you'll be alright...

So on you go, from day to day,
from now till then, if all goes well,
with any fun that you can find,
you live your life in your small World
as if you'd lived here all you life.

Of course – you'll feel much more secure
if you never *really* think
about the way things *really are...*

In re Darkness, Goblins etc

You'd laughed at all your childhood fears
when you grew up and left behind
those horrid goblins on dark stairs,
you thought you knew they don't exist,
the dark was safe, or so you said.

But now you're in the PBI
and have to lead a night patrol,
or lay white tape in darkest black,
it won't be goblins waiting there
with guns, grenades and stuff like that.

The ruined house you have to clear,
with cellar steps down into void,
you wonder who is lurking there?
It's up to you, you must decide,
and quickly, what you have to do.

All this could maybe make you think
you might have been a bit too quick
to write off goblins and the like,
although, in practice, in the end,
that doesn't matter, not one bit.

You have to go, and that is that.

The evacuation of casualties, four to a jeep.

A Real Bed

I lay there thinking on the ground
and everything was diamond bright
as if I'd never seen before
or been asleep a month, a year.
I lay there thinking very hard.

I couldn't move my head at all
or stop it lolling to the left
it seemed my right arm wasn't there
and though as yet I felt no pain
I knew for certain I'd been hit.

I must admit to no surprise
four nights before I'd dreamt this scene
of being wounded at first light
but then I woke before I knew
what happened at the very end.

We'd been the link with airborne troops
so now their wounded could go back
and on my stretcher I lay still
beside a ruined tennis court
till my turn came at half-past four.

And while I lay, things came and went,
I coughed a bit and up came blood.
I knew my strength was going fast
and though I thought it very odd,
it didn't seem to matter much.

They put my stretcher on a jeep
but found that underneath it lay
a little lake of clot and blood,
dripped from an undetected wound
on to the loose red tennis ash.

That night I reached a tented ward
across the gentle River Rhine
all nicely cleaned and given jags
and with my bonnet and my badge
beside my nice new stretcher 'bed'.

That stretcher now was my small world
where umpteen pillows propped me up
(a 'chest case' never, ever, lies)
for five more endless days, I think
of drowsy dreams and jags and jags.

One dawn they came to fly us home,
at Brussels' stop they took me off,
they said they thought I wouldn't 'do',
'the hospital would take me in',
but cobbles shook me all apart.

When I got there the place was full
with people lying outside the wards,
but when the QA came along
this brilliant woman found a bed,
my own, my really proper bed.

5th Bn Cas. 26/3/45: Hamminkeln, 0330–0700 hrs 2 ORs killed in action – Lt DC Simpson (Bn IO)
and 3 ORs wounded.

QA: a Nursing Sister of the Queen Alexandra's Imperial Military Nursing Service.
The hospital which took me in was most probably Hôpital Saint-Pierre, rue Haute.

A DC3 Dakota
'they put me on a plane again'.

The Gift

In Brussels they were kind to me,
they trimmed my wounds, they sewed me up,
they told me I'd had all the luck
and when a peaceful week had passed,
they put me on a plane again.

From plane to train, to Derby Royal,
into a little twelve-bed ward.
I learn to live with lots of pain,
and seeking sleep, try not to dream,
(the nurses tell me I am safe).

And there I learn the damage done
and how that jagged red-hot steel
had hit a lung, my ribs and nerves,
just missed great vessels in my neck,
(but only just by one hair's breadth).

And so, by rights, I should have died
(and though I knew I really lived)
it wasn't long before I saw
that in my life from that day on
that knowledge would be part of me.

In Derby I had peace to think,
to think about this life I had
(now every day's a bonus gift
and every gift a gift of life)
and in that life each day rejoice.

Before I'd been so close to death,
I'd learnt to live from day to day
and not expect to see the morn
but now the greatest gift I have
is giving welcome to each dawn.

I arrived at Derby Royal Infirmary in April 1945 and was discharged from active service, due to disability arising from wound, on 26/9/45.

One of 79th Arm'd Div's Crocodiles (flame thrower) in action.

They operated on me in the Brussels military hospital and then, a week or so later when I was fit to travel, they let me continue. A splinter of an 88mm shell had gone in my back, through my chest, coming out at my neck so I was a 'chest case' and had to be propped up – not easy on a stretcher.

We were flown from Brussels to an airfield near Watchfield and then taken to the train at Swindon. The train kept stopping as they took off a few casualties at all the major towns on our slow journey north; by 'spreading' us over the country they minimised the local impact of the large number of wounded at that time.

My account of that journey back to the UK from Brussels is a belated thank you to QAs for the wonderful care they took of us. I'm sorry if it sounds confused, we were all pretty heavily sedated. I think that most of the hundreds who made the same journey would have had a nightmare like mine when I fell asleep at last.

When I was unloaded from the ambulance train I discovered that my '*Somewhere*' was Derby.

A Passive Journey

A long, strange day. A noisy restless day, an endless day.
Stirring before six, a hurried meal,
taken from our beds, put back onto stretchers, goodbye to our nurses,
our stretchers loaded into ambulances and rattled fast over cobbles,
then rows of us waiting, waiting on our stretchers,
waiting in rows in the hanger; checked over but waiting.
Loaded again, loaded up into Dakotas of Transport Command,
their stores unloaded, now they are loaded with our stretchers,
the stretchers carry us, taking us out of here,
taking us somewhere else, somewhere other, not here.
The noise begins and with the noise the throbbing starts,
the shaking goes on, it goes with the noise, while the noise lasts.
A gentle landing, unloaded and loaded again into waiting ambulances,
no cobbles now just smooth roads to the railway, to the standing train,
still on our stretchers, they are loaded on to racks in the carriage, secured.
The QA checks us off from her list, she smiles at us, she calms us,
she smiles at me, there I am, lower rack on the right, still propped up,
still propped up with pillows on my stretcher,
lights are dimmed, we wait;
eventually the train pulls out, taking us somewhere.
Tired but can't sleep…
Night now, the train blacked-out, hot, stuffy, with its own hard rhythm,
not the drumming of the DC3 or the ambulance on those city cobbles
or that quiet smooth noise from the smooth roads,
but a harder noise, only hard noises now, sometimes a loud clatter,
the train rattles over points, through tunnels, stations,
growing louder, much louder, *louder as the rhythm changes,*
a deep threating noise and angry sounds from something tracked.
Near me a roaring noise, shouts and explosions, gunfire, small arms,
a flame-thrower is flaming, burning everything as it goes,
burning everything in its way with a roar of flame, flaring bright in the dark snow,
suddenly the wall of a burning house collapses into the road…
Now something has happened,
it is quite quiet, no noise, just quietness,
no sounds now, only quiet calm, a little shaded light again.
I am caught in the stillness of a train that has stopped somewhere.

The QA has her arm round me, gently cradling me against her,
she is talking quietly to me, telling me that now I am not there,
she tells me *now I am somewhere else. Somewhere, but not there.*

Derby Royal Infirmary. Officers' Ward April / May 1945.

I was taken off the train at Derby, and transferred to another ambulance, my third that day, which took me to the Royal Infirmary, I remember the orderly pushed the trolley with my stretcher on it up a long sloping corridor – feet first! The ward sister was the old style – firm (she had to be) but also kind and sympathetic. The nurses were also very good and the night nurses skilful in reassuring you if you woke from a nightmare. Like the others in that ward, I had nightmares frequently after I was wounded.

> *And then – in secret – in the dark*
> *life spins a web of nightmare thoughts,*
> > *of nightmare scenes,*
> *another piece of background to*
> *that stuff of dreams, our restless dreams.*

The Trick of Do-Not-Think-Ahead

Twelve of us lay in a twelve bed ward
(eleven'd been wounded, one had not)
and, by and large, and on the whole,
we seemed a fairly cheery lot,
(in spite of how things stood with us
in terms of pain and missing limbs
or damaged bits – that sort of stuff).

We joked and laughed and told tall tales
but never ever talked at all
about the problems facing us
when we got back to civvy life,
our need to feel quite safe again
and could we cope with being so young
when we had been so old, so long?

I didn't sleep well, because of pain,
and so had too much time to think.
I thought about the others there
and in particular two lads.
I wondered how life looked to them,
for both of them had lost both legs,
blown away above the knees.

Those two were very different types.
The one whose bed was close to me,
he rarely talked with anyone
and when his parents visited
he didn't speak,
he turned his back and faced the wall
and didn't speak.

The other was the 'life and soul'
and 'kept things going' in the ward.
He never moaned about himself
or how he'd drawn a shorter straw,
he organised our trips to pubs
(the wheelchairs pushed by those of us
with one good arm and two good legs).

I realised he used two tricks,
two tricks that in my past I'd used,
of Bashing-On-Regardless
and of Do-Not-Think-Ahead,
and so, like him, I took them up
(they'd worked for me in action,
they could work for me in peace).

I think perhaps I should explain
that if you Do-Not-Think-Ahead
you aren't so worried by your thoughts
of what might be (or not, in fact)
viz – would you suffer pain or death?
it frees your mind to do your job
while Bashing-On in an attack.

With those two tricks my fear was less,
the truth became quite clear to me:
I am alive, I should be dead,
so many friends didn't make it here.
When I am out things will be hard
but problems I have yet to meet
can never match those in my past.

Wedding day, 30/7/46.

Civvy Street

I came back home in 'forty-five,
(my stitches out, no dressings now)
awaiting discharge, I was told
but then I found I'd left behind
the confidence I used to have.
I feared that in the years ahead
I would not feel secure again
for every bang or slamming door
now sent me hurtling to the floor,
(I couldn't help it, though I tried).

In January of 'forty-six
I found the one and only girl
and she agreed to marry me
and right away she started work
to build me up and put my life
back on those rails that I'd been on.
She found the 'me' that I had been.
I lost my fear of sudden threat,
she helped me with the pain I had.
I loved that girl. She healed my life.

She held my hand and I was safe.

·

157 Brigade axis in Operation Blackcock, as it looked in 1987.

A Post-War Thought

I wonder if amongst those trees
that used to line that open road
that took so many to great pain
and others to such violent death,
I wonder if that simple shrine
is standing yet?

From His own anguish on His cross
the sadden'd Christ looked down on us,
in pity upon *Everyman*,
and on the many passers-by
who would not ever pass again,
that cold and snowy winter's day.

Those villages are now rebuilt,
their fields are cleared of mortar bombs
and life comes back to ravaged land,
but always in your heart of hearts
that anguish in their past remains,
and still the roads go on and on.

Corstorphine War Memorial.

Remembering Youth

The friends who died while we pressed on,
that trust in comrades that we had,
the way we lived life, as it was,
the things we saw, those things we did,
while we grew old when we were young.
We will remember while we live.

Old Men Standing

The old men stand, their heads are bowed,
so very still, a point of honour not to sway
or move their feet. The wind is cold.
They've gathered there and there they stand,
with campaign medals on their chests,
and do not sway or move their feet.

* * *

It's hard to see these men as young,
but young they were, though long ago,
well-trained and fit and keen and tough.
It's hard to think what life was like
for those men then, with wives, best girls
at home with tears, with fear, with love.

The old men stand, their minds are full
of such sad thoughts of their dead pals,
the friends they had to leave behind
who lie so still in their War Graves.
They also think of things they've seen,
those things they still have dreams about.

* * *

The seconds pass.

Those winds get colder every year,
old comrades stand, try not to sway,

I tense myself to keep quite still.

Remembrance

So many died, and of the rest
too many of us now have gone,
and those who live have grown old.
and men forget or never knew
and years roll on and much has changed;
so, while I could, I wrote these lines
for you to read and understand
and help to keep their memory young.

So that was why, and now that's done
and of our private, private world –
no trace remains that you could find
of those grey shapes on those straight roads,
and now there is no threat of death
there are no men with weapons there,
for all this happened, as you know,
so long, so very long ago.

I may, perchance, have said too much
but now I've done, I've had my say,
and told you where I'm coming from.
You've seen how fortunate I've been,
to have the chance to start again.

An Afterthought on Fireworks,
and Nice Old Men

About those times, now here's a thought,
most people who were in the line
don't speak about what happened there
and keep that as a private thing,
but *if they're startled it comes back,*
and if they're in the dark alone
and hear a noise or back door slam
or someone lets a firework off,
then they remember night patrols
or how old Laurie lost his life
or some black night they were attacked
and how – but that's enough of that,
quite soon they see there is no threat
and they are back with us again.

But that's a thought about old boys
on bonfire nights and nights like that;
those nice old chaps
who look so very calm and quiet.

An Afterthought on Not-Knowing

Often it was not-knowing-what
was going to be our next assault
and what was coming after that
and what about their next attack?
I mind that that was quite the thing
and so we just got used to that.

Our day-to-day was not-knowing-quite
about the noise you thought you heard
that came from somewhere in that wood?
about those dark shapes over there –
I couldn't make out – it wasn't clear –
but did they move and were you sure?

Most often it was not-knowing-who
would still be there at that day's end
or rather who-would-not be there,
which ones amongst us would we lose?
and though you knew it wouldn't be you,
you-really-knew that wasn't quite true.

But, looking back these sixty years,
I see that time when I grew up
showed me the way to curb my mind –
not let my thoughts go racing on
down scary routes, but think about
those Things-I-know, the Love-I-hold.

It wasn't easy learning how
but that's what mattered
at the
End.

DAVID SIMPSON spent a month in Germany immediately after leaving school in the summer of 1938, an unusual experience for a Scots lad in those pre-war days. On the return journey from the Bavarian Alps, he visited Munich (the 'Capital of the Movement') and the Party Stadium in Nuremberg during the week before the Nazi Rally; a few days later, in Frankfurt, he wandered into the Jewish quarter and saw the conditions there. After that experience it was perhaps not surprising that, when the 'September Crisis' arose some three weeks after his return to Edinburgh, he should join a local Territorial unit, The 4/5 Battalion The Royal Scots, as a private.

He was wounded in March 1945 while serving with the 5th Battalion HLI, and as a result was discharged in October of that year. As one of many unpleasant consequences of being wounded, he found that he had become a very unsettled and anxious individual. The recovery of sufficient self-confidence to enable him to complete an Honours degree and a subsequent post-graduate degree was entirely due to the support he received from his wife Isobel; they were married in 1946, at the end of his first year at Edinburgh University.

His wartime verses have come as a great surprise to him. As he says, he is not really a 'poetry person' and has no idea why they should have started to emerge so suddenly, a couple of years after the death of his wife and some fifty-five years after the events they portray. At the end of March each year he sends Easter flowers to the Evangelische Kirche in Hamminkeln, the little town where he was wounded, as an individual act of reconciliation.

David Simpson was born in Corstorphine, Midlothian, in 1920, and lives in Edinburgh. He was awarded the MBE in 1966. The portrait on the back cover is by his grandson, David James C. Simpson.